Princess Mani

Divine Connection Stories

and

Tools for Synchronicities and Miracles

**Divine Connection Stories and
Tools for Synchronicities and Miracles**
Princess Mani

ISBN: 978-0-9914993-6-6

Photographs by the author unless otherwise noted.
Layout and pre-press by Lighthouse24

Table of Contents

*This book is dedicated to
Ascended Master Teachers
including Jesus, Mother Mary,
King Solomon, St. Germaine
and many others.*

Introduction

Earlier in life, I remember seeking to understand why things happened, and learning the lessons from life's events. Every experience is an opportunity to learn lessons and gain wisdom. Once I learned that everything in life has purpose and that there are no coincidences, the quickening of finding my true self happened.

Guidance began to flow in, a reconnection to my soul, and then knowing of my higher self happened. Next, the synchronistic experiences that served to guide me and confirm my intuitive knowledge occurred. Being in the flow felt like a brand new way of living, freedom, light and bliss.

Following this intuitive process led me to my purpose-driven life. Each person has been wired for this path. Once you begin to connect to soul and higher self, you begin to know which step to take, set intentions, create, take action and then manifest part of your divine plan. Living life this way is the life of synchronicities and miracles.

It is all available to you, but you must clear the blocks and reconnect to your soul and higher self. Then you arrive at the moment of knowing who you are and why you came. This means that there is so much more available to you than you ever knew existed. No more monotony, regrets and depression;

only newness, learning and excitement. Imagine awaking each day like a child at Christmas. You are that child, ready to open the gifts of the present day.

With connection to higher self, it is Christmas every day. When you remember who you are, it all begins to unfold. Open your heart, clear the mind, trust your soul, and have more faith – faith that can move mountains.

In this book, I am sharing with you short stories of actual events that occurred in my life recently, stories of synchronicities and little miracles. Then you will learn about tools or shortcuts, to be in the flow of synchronicities and miracles so that you can manifest your higher life purpose.

We are all destined to experience awesome and amazing higher life purpose; it is a matter of choosing to take the next step. We are creating humanity's Heaven on Earth. Remember your unique, important role. Ask to know your next specific higher life purpose. Once you know, build it with all of your abilities and gifts. You have everything you need within, and more will come through you to give you the empowerment and to build your faith so you can manifest it.

I AM wishing you blessings on your journey of experiencing synchronicities and creating miracles.

Princess Mani

A Divine Eagle Rescue Story

Hello my name is Princess Mani, the humble princess of God who is in total control of the mind and who knows no defeat. Mani means master of the mind, one who makes the impossible possible. When you too have mastered the mind, you will experience the impossible. We just call it divine flow.

The stories of beloved Princess Mani tell about divine experiences and knowledge, and are meant to be shared with all the children of the world. Let life unfold the beauty and mysteries of knowing the unknown and seeing the unseen through the soul-connected eyes of the beholder.

The great eagle is one of the most important animal spirits. It symbolizes courage, strength, freedom, loyalty, wisdom, faith, perspective and connection with higher power. The eagle teaches us to have faith in our purpose.

January 10, 2013 was one of those special days that you think is the most special day of your life! It was worth the two hours of making endless calls, following the bird, losing sight of the bird for twenty minutes, finding the bird just in time for arrival of the rescue team. It was an amazing experience to see this bird paddling in the water with its wings for 50 meters, steady and focused, directly to us and landing ashore at our feet; it was trusting enough to ask and receive help from humans.

When I arrived at the park and sat on the bench, it was 11:30 a.m. There was a large blue heron just standing in the water, staring in my direction for awhile. That is not the usual direction to be searching for fish. Then there was an osprey that circled over head, looking at me when it got close. Then a second one took a turn at it. They were not fishing, but were sending messages. There were many supernatural lights around me that were beaconing this incredible creature twenty minutes before my friend arrived. I was fascinated with the lights myself and was busy capturing the images. Within five minutes of my friend's arrival, she noticed the movement in the water. It looked like a giant sea turtle paddling directly toward us. As it got closer, it looked like a falcon. We went to the water's edge and it slowly walked right up to us. It was looking directly into our eyes for help. This bird was on a mission, communicated to us, and was determined to succeed! We noticed it was weak and had a badly damaged beak. It was too weak to fly, probably could not catch prey, but managed to cross Safety Harbor paddling with its wings. A man came by to help, and he said it was a golden eagle. That is what makes the story even more amazing.

We called many places trying to get someone to rescue the bird. It took some time to reach the people who could help and for them to drive over to the park. The Suncoast Seabird Sanctuary said it was most likely a juvenile bald eagle. When a few people gathered around the bird to take pictures, it walked away into the trees for shelter. We lost sight of the bird for twenty minutes. It was at that time I got a message that the sheriff officers were on the road headed to the park. The pressure was on to locate this creature. We knew it could not have gone too far in its weakened state. The three of us must have walked by it numerous times. I thought to myself, *think like the bird, move like the bird*. I looked in the shadows of the retaining wall and found it huddled in the foliage. It camouflaged so well.

After two hours, two sheriff officers and a wildlife rescue person arrived on the scene. The bird was in a weakened condition and had been so patient waiting for the help to arrive. They handled him well and the bird was trusting. The rescue team did a great job of getting a gentle hold of the juvenile bald eagle.

It's beyond words, the feeling of being directly communicated to by an eagle, observing the gentle grace of this bird while
waiting for help to arrive, and the manner in which it received
help from the rescue team. As we said goodbye, I looked at the
bird and his eyes were looking directly into mine. Love, faith and
hope shined through at its best today.

Enjoy the picture of loving, green divine lights shining
through the sunset which I took that evening at Honeymoon
Island.

Princess Mani

Stories of Divine Messenger Birds

Birds are divine messengers to humans. Observe what birds cross your path and look for the message they bring to you. This will help you gain insight into the things happening in your life and guide you with your life purpose.

The hummingbird is a little bird with a great amount of spirit. It invites more joy, love and healing into your life. It has mastered balance, for it has sensibility and power. Its wings move in an infinity or figure-8 pattern which allows it to move quickly with great flexibility in different directions as well as to hover in place.

I most resonate to this feathered creature. It is my spirit essence, that is, if I were a bird. Maybe I am part hummingbird for its spirit is within me. Maybe you feel closeness to a specific type of bird. It is the spirit we connect to. On a trip to Sedona, I was taking a picture of a hummingbird feeder as it was pleasing to the eyes. As I was taking the picture, a hummingbird managed to fly toward the bird feeder into the view, then turn around and fly away. It was a joyful, unexpected gift.

Before and during a time of life change, I was noticing the raven. The raven is an intelligent bird and its presence indicates a time for change. It symbolizes the mind, and an ability to *intuit* information rather than *seek* for information. Trust your inner wisdom and intuition, for it will reveal deep mysteries. The raven appeared one morning in the front yard, then twice again while traveling in Sedona. I was sitting in the outdoor patio of a restaurant when the raven flew in and landed on the roof. It was cawing quite loudly with purpose. I had to step outside to take a look at the bird. It was after that experience that I looked up the meaning of the raven and understood the message. After I fully understood the message, the raven stopped appearing. I learned to trust that the answers I did not have at the moment would come to me by intuition and I did not have to look for them from outside sources.

Birds are divine messengers to humans. Observe what birds cross your path and look for the messages they bring to you. This will help you gain insight into the things happening in your life and guide you with your life purpose.

The blue heron carries the message of self-determination and wisdom. They maneuver through life and co-create their own circumstances. They remind you to follow the heart and the wisdom within, instead of doing what others tell you to do; for you know what is best. When you follow your heart, you will soar like the blue herons. This message came to life in the form of a pair of blue herons last winter. My friend and I were sitting on the bench at the park in deep discussion about the things we were guided to do. At that moment, we saw two blue herons fly from the right to the left, out of the field for less than twenty seconds then return to view flying from the left to the right. We laughed for joy when they came out again from the right into our view and flew up and away into the sky. It was a beautiful and enjoyable experience to receive this message from a pair of elegant, synchronized blue herons.

Then it was the woodpecker that entered occasionally for a few months, flying into a tree close by and getting right to work pecking on that tree. Many times it would have a red cap of feathers on its head. It brings the message of opportunities, progress and protection. The woodpecker reminds us to be mindful of our words, to ourselves as well as to others.

The eagle appeared as a spirit guide in January 2013 and for-ever touched my heart. It is written in the Eagle Rescue Story. The bald eagle symbolizes spiritual power and illumination. The eagle brings forth the inner child and this powerful energy supports in healing and creating. The sign of the eagle indicates new vision will open. What a beautiful gift – to awaken and see life through the eyes of an eagle.

The wild turkey appeared on Easter to bring a message. I did not even know there were turkeys in urban Florida until that day. I was less than a mile away from my friend's house when 20 meters ahead of me, I saw a turkey on the left side of the road stepping down the curb and beginning to cross the road. I stopped the car and made sure no one was behind me and pulled out my camera to take this unusual turkey crossing. By the time I took the photo, the turkey had stepped onto the curb on the right side of the road. It walked so elegantly and took its time.

Apparently turkeys can walk extremely fast as well as fly, but it intentionally walked very slowly and purposely. I could see the turkey's distinct red neck, head and wattle. The turkey brings the message of blessings, abundance and thanks giving.

The blue jay has appeared so many times in the past few months that I take its message to heart. I would step outside and one would fly in and out of view or I would be looking out the window and one would fly into view. A few times, a blue jay would fly right in front of the car so I would see it through the windshield. They must have GPS because they time it just right so they don't get hit, but they can get so close to send their message. Once you notice the blue jay, it is flying off to do its other things. The blue jay symbolizes an open heart, clear mind and pure soul. Its message is assertiveness, determination and fearlessness. It prompts the beholder to develop and use innate divine royal abilities.

The cardinals have appeared three times in the past month in different locations. The most notable sighting was while driving the car. One red cardinal flew in front of the windshield and right behind him was another cardinal. The cardinal's message brings cheer, renewal, confidence and the ability to tap into creativity. It reminds us to recognize ourselves as important and everything we do is important.

The mockingbird has appeared both at home and a few other places. The bird in the backyard sings calls of many birds, hours on end, and sometimes at night. Just the other evening the mockingbird was out in the front yard when I came home. It wanted to be noticed and so I did stop to listen. It sings loudly and beautifully with a brilliant repertoire of different bird sounds, but its brown body is hard to see as it is well camouflaged in the tree. It has a rather plain outer appearance, but it shows white patches on its shoulders when the wings are outstretched. This has an effect on others nearby.

The mockingbird brings the message of joy, gratitude, protection, security and power of song and voice. It connects you to find your sacred song, life's purpose and special gifts. Mockingbird also hears the true song of others. This divine bird reminds you that intuition and creativity will lead you to success. Keep this message of the mockingbird close to your heart, for it is sacred.

Lastly is the message of the swans. A few days ago at a beloved friend's home, we sat by the pond and the swans came by to send us their love and message. One of the swans came first, looked at us, then it swam from side to side honoring us. Then the other joined in, and the pair of swans swam synchronized from side to side, directly in front of us at the water's edge. When they were done with synchronized swimming, they put their heads close together in a gesture of affection. This picture

I captured and share with you. Swans' message is love, grace, elegance, beauty, purity, transformation, and partnership or union. Allow more of your inner powerful beauty to awaken and transform into your outer world.

Princess Mani

Stories of Divine Doves

Birds are special creatures that carry celestial messages for humans. Notice them and their meanings to receive the guidance they carry.

When I moved into my divinely guided home, there was a pair of mourning doves on the ground by the front door to greet me. I knew this would be the sanctuary I had been seeking and guided to. Doves are a symbol of love, peace and the Holy Spirit.

Many times I would look out the window after hearing the cooing sound of doves and see a pair of doves in the tree outside the window.

It was one blessed Sunday when I was in front of the house and looked up to see a large dove above the garage. It looked at me and became glowing with a golden sphere, like a halo encircling it. My friend was there too and stared at it in amazement. It was my first time seeing a golden-haloed dove, and in its presence I felt blessed by the light. This beautiful exchange of energy lasted several minutes and time stood still.

The day I was preparing to travel abroad, a dear friend called and while on the phone, I noticed three doves in the tree by the window. After the phone call, I went outside to see them and was surprised because now there were eight doves. They looked pretty comfortable even as I approached closer to count them, so

I thought to get my camera from inside the house. When I came out, there were now six doves. In that moment, I knew it as a message of the numbers 3-8-6.

I looked up the meaning of each number and then as a whole in Doreen Virtue's book *Angel Numbers 101: The Meaning of 111, 123, 444 and Other Number Sequences*. Three signifies the Ascended Masters are responding to your prayers. Eight represents abundance and prosperity, infinite flow for your life purpose. Six reminds you not to worry about finances and to trust that your prayers will be answered. The message of angel number 386 is to release all financial cares to the Ascended Masters as the Ascended Masters are supporting you in all ways.

Additionally, I took the message to mean the following. Believe that all you need will come to you. Trust that you have within you all that you need to manifest your higher desires. Focus on your life purpose and your financial needs will be met. The angels, guides and Ascended Masters are helping you manifest what you need to allow you to progress on with your life purpose. Trust and have faith that can move mountains! They are working to bring you what you need so you can do your teaching, healing and humanitarian works. Remember you deserve this help so that you are better able to help others. What a beautiful orchestration by the doves with the divine presence. It was a divinely guided message that I needed and allowed me to let go of any cares regarding this.

A few months later, I was asked to participate in a crystal bowl sound healing event and give healing energy to the group. It was at a large warehouse building and quite hot inside so I stepped out to get fresh air, center and connect to my higher self. As I stepped out to the landing, a ring-necked dove flew in and landed on the electric line above me. It made eye contact and stayed around. I noticed it had a black collar around the neck and a pale colored, almost white body. This variety is not commonly seen here. I felt gifted by grace from this divine messenger dove. With this energy, I walked back in and experi- enced a new expanded presence of the angels sending love and light energy around the room, creating a vortex of beautiful energy.

The combination of crystal bowl sound and healing energy was awesome and all those present were touched. After the sound healing, a woman who was pregnant came to give thanks, for she knew her baby received the energy too. Raising the vibration like this clears blocked energy for a healing and allows you to better connect to your higher self.

These past few months have been filled with many changes, the days are quickening, new experiences are hap- pening and energy is increasing within and around the planet. As I was driving home from work, feeling joy and appreciating the scenery of the Gulf of Mexico, I looked up to see a white dove fly by the windshield, high enough not to be hit, but close enough not to be missed. It was pure white with dove tail feathers too. Divinity, purity and love was the message carried by this bird.

Sometimes the energy exchange can go the other way. I had an experience of a dove wanting to receive energy from me. I was at the park and noticed a dove fly into a tree where a larger dove was contently resting on a branch close to the trunk of the tree. The small dove flew away as I stopped in front of the tree. The larger dove took notice and became more alert. I sent the dove love, saying "I love you, I love you, I love you." It got happy, turned toward me and walked on the branch about a meter out to get closer. Then it looked at me, received the energy, turned its head to the side in a gesture of love and compassion. I sent it gratitude and love for the exchange of energy.

The most recent story is the best and saved for last. A few days later, from inside my house, I saw a dove outside on the tree. It was graceful, gentle and loving. I reached for my camera and took photos. As I was taking them, I noticed the colors of super luminescent blues – turquoise and royal blues. The area around the dove appeared white in three adjoined lobes. The white area also looks like a dove. I knew that it represented the trinity, the Holy Spirit.

All of my photos of the dove came out in the super luminescent blue spectrum. Never before had I seen this. Even the inside of the window pane and window frame, which is a pale yellow, turned blue. It was truly an experience of being graced by the Holy Spirit. The divine lights of the Ascended Masters were sending blue lights which represent energy, strength and power. In this picture I share with you, focus on it to receive the Ascended Masters' energy, strength and power for assisting you in manifesting your highest desires and feel the blessings of hope, faith and love.

The doves remind us that we have the divine creative ability to create amazing lives. Know that the divine creative powers are within you, and enjoy the manifestation of your life's story.

I wish you success on your journey, on your divine life path. Connect to the beauty and divine in all things, meditate on this blessed picture, observe the messenger birds around you, listen to and follow your intuition as you are creating your divine life story, which will quicken your path to more joy and love light.

Princess Mani

A Story of an Unusual, Intelligent, Divine Sweet Potato and Three Friends

This organic sweet potato was purchased in the beginning of September, 2012. I had left my job in early September to follow in a new direction, taking that leap of faith that had been calling my name. I remember while I was still at my old job, I talked to a client about this sweet potato I had at home that wanted to grow and continue to live. It was the only one that I had ever seen grow substantial stalks from its buds. This client had been an experienced gardener and told me that you can grow many sweet potato plants by slicing off the buds and planting them in the soil. I was trying to explain to her that this sweet potato was growing without soil or water. She could not give me an explanation of it other than they have a lot of energy stored in them.

When my parents came to visit during the third week of September, they brought my old Virginia Tech mug. It was a tall, skinny mug, perfect to hold this sweet potato. So there it was placed and left to be. The following months consumed all of my attention as I was trying to create a new business. I did not pay much attention to the sweet potato, as I also had two long trips during this time. Months later, I was amazed at how healthy, green and happy it looked. No water and no soil had been given to it. It was the works of the angels is what I thought, for it was receiving a lot of super natural energy. I did not want to do anything to it for I would have to take responsibility for its demise if I fiddled with it. I wouldn't know whether to put the whole thing in soil or soak it in water. I usually do not have a green thumb and what energy source was sustaining it was doing a perfect job.

When friends would visit, they would notice the sweet potato, which made me pay more attention to how it had been growing. I started taking more notice of it in February and began to take occasional photos. So I have photos from February onward. There is no sign of it diminishing its existence. All of the original leaves are still there and more are appearing. It is radiant, loving and amazing.

How can a sweet potato grow without water or soil? It gets plenty of sunshine during the day through the upper windows. The solar energy is captured by the chlorophyll in the leaves and by the process of photosynthesis the energy that it needs is produced. Based on the looks of it, the plentiful green leaves help it transform the solar energy and sustain its vitality. We can sense from observation how much solar energy is captured by this sweet potato and how it can convert enough energy to sustain it for at least a year.

The two children who have come to visit a few times since February have grown fond of this plant. They wished to have a sweet potato plant too. So I bought four sweet potatoes to see which ones would be theirs. Three of the sweet potatoes started growing stalks at two weeks. By the time the children saw them, they had been in my home for three to four weeks. The three sweet potatoes were starting to grow a little bit at that time and the children wanted to put crystals around them to make them grow faster.

These children are a quick study as I had just finished telling them about placing a few quartz crystals at the base of two small Christmas cactus plants. They were still in their original plastic pots from a year and a half ago. Somehow they were still holding on to life without much care, but when I placed the crystals in the tray that held them, within a week and a half, there were new light green leaves that had formed and all of the leaves had a beautiful shine to them. They were glowing with energy and health from the addition of the crystal energy.

These three newer sweet potatoes had been named Happy, Cliff and Star by the children. Happy had two stalks, like it is holding both arms up in joy. Cliff had one stalk that looked like it might be hanging on with all its might at the edge of a cliff. Star had six buds growing stalks, like a six pointed star. Star was growing slower and steadier, conserving energy because it had six stalks to give energy to, compared to two or one. Star was not in a competition to grow as fast as possible, but was focused to be a beautiful, balanced star. So Star was growing slowly and steadily.

I told the children they could pick up the sweet potato plants when they gained more energy and were a little bigger. Of course they wanted to pick them up the next day. The children told their mother that they wished they could see the sweet potatoes and thought about them daily. The sweet potato friends were growing so rapidly, nearly doubling their height in a week. One of Happy's stalks was almost as tall as the sweet potato plant that had been growing for eight months. It briefly crossed my mind that it was too incredible, the rate of Happy and Cliff's growth.

Something a little upsetting happened to Happy and Cliff a week after the children's visit. It looked like there was a segment about an inch from the top of the stalks that had dried and turned brown. The section above it had not died yet but was bound to do so soon, as its lifeline was cut off from below. Below the dried out section, all looked healthy. The new buds growing out of the stalk to form new leaves were active. A week and a half after the downturn, it looked like they were going to make it, and it happened for a good reason. There was a balancing act lesson much like the moral of the story about the tortoise and the hare. There was no more competition and they learned to mature at the rate that best served them, to conserve some energy, to learn to adapt and to stay in balance.

It seems the plant's intelligence knew it was too fast – that it could not sustain itself at that growth. It halted, slowed down, repaired itself and found a new way. Maybe the combination of the crystals around it and the children sending it their super charged love energy helped it grow super fast. I felt there was a competition between Cliff and Happy as to who could grow the tallest to please the children. I could tell Star was not a part of that competition and stayed the course.

These sweet potatoes teach us a few lessons about life. They are sensitive to our energy and consciousness. They have the adaptability to grow in different ways, find a way to live without water, soil or minerals. The leaves are numerous and growing, but are folded to retain moisture. The sweet potatoes communicate with the heart of the children and adults, but especially the children who have that pure, open heart. We each want to be loved, but we have to stay true to ourselves, stay in balance as energy shifts around us. Energy, whether from the sun or hearts of children or angels, helps to create beautiful, blessed creations. Know that there is brilliant energy and love all around us, and in knowing so, it is.

Princess Mani

Divine Love and the Violet Flame

We are love, we are divine. Purify yourselves so that love is the resonance of your being – feel love, think loving thoughts, act lovingly to yourself and others. This is the original state in which we were created. We are given great powers to create with our divine, love energy. We can begin to heal ourselves with love and help to heal others by giving unconditional love. Purify your mind, body and spirit to return all that is not in resonance with love back to love. We are crystal vessels of liquid light that are connected to our higher selves. You may have heard the term I AM Presence. It is synonymous with the divine within and higher self. We are all divine, created in the image and similitude as The Divine. There is great empowerment when we remember the truth.

It is our love energy that is used to create all higher things for our higher desires. If you get stuck and need a tool to clear negativity which allows for more love energy to resonate, use the mighty Violet Flame. Decree that the Violet Flame release the negative energy at hand, stay positive and in the light. Visualize the Violet Flame swirling through you, others and the negative thoughts, emotions and actions, and transmuting negative energy back into the light of love.

The Violet Flame has been given to us by the Ascended Masters as a powerful gift to clear negativity from the world. Begin within, and use it to clear the negative thoughts, feelings, words and actions you may have and any negativity from the past your being is responsible for. Then expand outward and send it to those who are experiencing negativity and affecting others in negative ways. This helps to release negative energy and return to the state of loving energy and balance. It is a flame that swirls around and through the negative energy to transmute it to a higher vibration. Notice how effective a tool it is and the immediate effects it has on creating peace and harmony. This is a beneficial tool for all children of God, regardless of age.

When we purify our minds of all negative thought patterns and negative emotions and also open our hearts to receive and give divine love, we become connected to all. This is when you are connected to your mighty I AM Presence. We can then know the unknown and see the unseen. We can ask and the answer will be given to us.

I share with you this beautiful divine gift that is a gift for all children of the world. The Violet Flame, used as a powerful tool, will help you on your higher life path and help to remove the obstacles within you and around you. Success is guaranteed when you see the divine within you and around you and quickly choose to release all that is not.

You can release all types of negative energies with the Violet Flame. It will accelerate the process like no other tool, a most blessed gift indeed. Your divine love light shines through and brings healing, joy and the energy to create everything and anything your pure heart and mind desire.

Infinite Blessings,
Princess Mani

Colors and Crystals

Receive light, send out light and so it goes. Colors are given to us with purpose. If we examine our energy body, we see that it carries all of the colors of the rainbow. In the body, there are seven energy chakras or energy centers spinning like wheels, and each chakra has a different energy frequency that creates a corresponding color of the rainbow. Red is the color at the base of the spine and violet is the color at the crown.

The colors we wear in our clothing and jewelry, as well as the colors that we surround ourselves with in our homes, definitely affect us. Do you know how to use them with purpose? ROYGBIV has to do with energy frequencies. When all those colors are combined, they form white light. Light rays carry messages. They affect how you feel and can affect how others around you feel. Choose and use colors to your joy and benefit.

Princess Mani has studied design at two universities. She decorates her home with a balance of colors, elements and crystals and has art work with images of divine animals and sacred symbols. They lift the energy vibration of her home.

Images like birds, butterflies and flowers raise the energy vibration. The rose flower symbolizes love and sends out the vibration of love. Divine love is the highest energy vibration in the Universe. Birds carry divine messages and butterflies carry the message of soul, grace and transformation. As we expand our consciousness, we can expand the energy of our home and our inner and outer world.

Crystals give great energy as they resonate at frequencies of several million times per second. Having crystals in the home will raise the energy vibration, increase health, harmony and prosperity. *How do you know which crystals to choose?* They will choose you if you set the intention of choosing the right one for you and allow your inner guidance to choose. As you hold a crystal in your hand, feel for the energy it is sending you. If you feel its energy and like it, that crystal would especially benefit you.

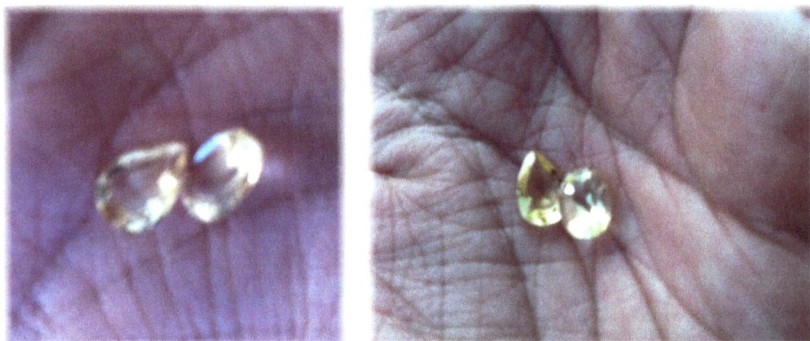

Amethyst, rose quartz and quartz crystals are my favorites to have in the home and wear as jewelry. The quartz crystal can be used during prayer or meditation to help manifest your desires by holding it in your hand. Amethyst is one of the most powerful healing crystals. The violet color symbolizes communication with the higher self. It gives the energy to help increase intuition and healing. Rose quartz has the energy of love. You may want to have a small bowl of rose quartz to maximize the love energy in your home or office. These crystals work on the surrounding space.

If you place a quartz crystal by a plant, it will assist to increase the plant's growth and glow. See its effects and know how quickly it does change. Crystals have been used since ancient days and we are reconnecting to their benefits. They are the divine gifts from Mother Earth. Experiment with crystals, keep an open mind and heart and experience the beautiful energy expanding around you.

I have my crystals blessed by angels. You can do this too. Just ask for the angels and divine presence to bless crystals for whatever you are wishing. I usually ask for love, joy, protection, health, prosperity, and guidance. Enjoy the feeling of the extra glow and flow in you and in your home. This will affect all who are in your home, including pets and plants, as well as all of the people with whom you connect.

The color white carries all rays of colors. It increases your energy outward so it helps you draw in the flow you want in your life. This expanded energy outward helps you connect to the people and things on your higher path. When you want to feel a different mood, you can use colors to help. Also, the colors you wear affect those who see you. What color vibrations are you sending out today?

- White is the color of purity and wisdom. White brightens any room, increases healing and raises the energy vibration.

- Red is associated with boldness and heat.

- Pink is the color of love and compassion.

- Orange stimulates enthusiasm and promotes creativity.

- Yellow increases self-esteem, joy and well-being.

- Green promotes health, balance, change and growth.

- Blue is the color of truth, harmonious expansion, serenity and open verbal communication

- Indigo is the color of intelligence, wisdom and intuition.

- Violet color purifies, removes obstacles, inspires the imagination and connects you to your higher self. It is the color of purpose.

Raise your vibration and manifest your intentions with the use of color choices and crystal presence. This will help you to heal, release any negative energy around, protect you and guide you on your life purpose.

To all children of the world, let your light shine bright.

Princess Mani

High Vibration Foods

Energy is our greatest resource, not time or money. With more energy, we can creative abundance; with more energy, we can have better health; and with more energy, we can make better use of time. How do we access more energy?

It begins with the food choices we make. Does the food you are choosing to eat have the bio-energy that our human bodies can utilize? Plants have converted solar energy into useable form; we then take the plant energy and convert it to our useable energy. Remember that the sun is our planet's energy source and that the plants have a greater amount of bio-energy.

Can you imagine how simple eating would be if there was one plant that contained all of the nutrients one needs? Can you imagine how much extra free time you would have and how much more energetic you could be?

The best way to prepare food is to eat it raw. There are many options for eating raw food. You can chop it up and add other vegetables, spices, herbs, nuts and fruits. It can be put into a blender to make soups and smoothies. If plant protein, like hemp seeds are added, it could be a complete meal in one cup. This way of preparation allows all of the nutrients available in the fruits and vegetables to be ingested. When food is micro-waved or cooked over 118 degrees Farenheit, the enzymes are lost and nutrients are reduced. The longer the cooking and the more water exposure, the more the nutrients are lost. Canned foods have lost some nutrients and processed foods have lost even more nutrients. We have come a long way since hunting and gathering times, but whole, fresh and minimal processing was, and still is, healthier.

Another reason to have raw plant foods in the diet is that their enzymes support digestion. Once cooked, even chopped or blended and left more than twenty minutes, the food enzymes begin to be lost due to oxidation. Try to include some organic raw plant foods in your daily diet.

Learn to use herbs and spices with your foods to stimulate your taste buds and to provide health benefits. Try a new spice or herb every so often and learn its benefits. Did you know that cumin seeds have iron, digestive and cancer prevention benefits? Cumin has been used in ancient Egypt, Greece, Rome and is now used all around the world. I want to mention a few more. Vanilla bean has antioxidant, anti-inflammatory and cognition enhancing benefits. Cinnamon has anti-oxidant, antimicrobial, blood sugar control and blood pressure control benefits. Oregano is a healthy herb for it has antioxidant, antibacterial, anti-inflammatory benefits and nutrients including vitamin K. Cilantro is an herb with anti-inflammatory, antioxidant, anti-septic, digestive, immune boosting, blood sugar lowering, endocrine stimulating and detoxification benefits. Remember to spice up your food for flavor and health.

Anything unnatural the body ingests or breathes in that cannot be used, the body tries to eliminate. These are considered toxins by the body. If enough toxins collect, then the body treats them as stressors. This causes inflammation and can trigger the disease process. Make conscious, healthy choices and know why you are eating the foods you have chosen. Experiment with methods of food preparation that allow you to access the most nutrients that are available in the whole food. Making healthy food choices is a work in progress, improves with practice and then becomes a healthy habit.

I hope this food for thought will inspire you to try something new in your kitchen. Try existing healthy recipes or create new recipes that do not over process the nutritious foods you have chosen.

Once you realize that it is all about energy, and that we are energy, you begin the journey to expand your energy, expand your consciousness, expand your choices, and expand your life experiences and possibilities.

Bon Appetite!
Princess Mani

Princess Mani Ultra Healthy and Super Delicious Smoothie Recipe (one serving)

Ingredients:
- One small handful of frozen organic blueberries, buy fresh then wash and freeze or buy frozen
- One small handful of frozen organic cranberries, buy fresh then wash and freeze if frozen not available
- One Banana
- $^1/_2$ cup hemp milk (or flax milk or almond milk)
- 3 Tablespoons of organic vanilla or plain yogurt
- Dash of organic vanilla
- Dash of organic cinnamon
- Two Tablespoons organic hemp seeds

Mix all ingredients except for the hemp seeds in a blender until smooth, then add two Tablespoon of hemp seeds and mix. Pour into a glass or crystal cup and enjoy!

Amazing and Beautiful Quinoa Salad (two servings)

Ingredients:
- 1 cup Tri-Color Quinoa
- 2 cups water
- $1^1/_2$ cups finely-chopped organic red cabbage
- $^3/_4$ cup lightly-chopped organic mini orange, yellow, red peppers
- $^1/_4$ teaspoon salt
- $^1/_4$ teaspoon black pepper
- $^1/_2$ teaspoon oregano
- $^1/_2$ teaspoon cumin
- $^1/_3$ cup lightly-chopped organic cilantro
- 2 cups lightly-chopped organic super greens like spinach, red and green Swiss chard, arugula
- Salsa or guacamole to enhance the dish

Rinse 1 cup of Tri-Color Quinoa.

Bring 2 cups of water and 1 cup of Tri-Color Quinoa to a boil on medium-high heat, reduce heat to medium-low, cover and simmer 10-15 minutes until water is absorbed. Remove from heat with lid closed.

While the Quinoa is cooking, wash all vegetables, then finely chop $1^1/_2$ cups of red cabbage, chop $^3/_4$ cup mini orange, yellow and red peppers, and lightly chop $^1/_3$ cup cilantro.

Once the Quinoa is finished cooking, in a large frying pan, on medium heat, add 2 Tablespoons olive oil, sauté $1^1/_2$ cups of red cabbage for one minute, add $^3/_4$ cup lightly chopped mini orange, yellow, red peppers, and stir. Add $^1/_4$ teaspoon salt, $^1/_4$ teaspoon black pepper, $^1/_2$ teaspoon oregano, $^1/_2$ teaspoon cumin. Fluff the Quinoa and lightly stir it into the vegetables then turn off the heat and remove the pan from the heat. Lastly, add $^1/_3$ cup chopped cilantro and 2 cups of lightly chopped super greens like spinach, red and green Swiss chard, arugula (any one or all is fine), stir lightly.

Total cooking time for vegetables is only about three minutes. Enjoy this super healthy, quick and easy to make meal-in-one with a spoonful of salsa or guacamole served on top.

Blessing
Food and Water

What happens when we bless the food and water? Why do we do this? Many people do this to give thanks for the meal, and to make our bodies healthier. We may all want to consider doing this blessing every single time we bring anything to be consumed into our bodies.

Have you heard about Masaru Emoto's studies on the effects words have on water that was crystallized into snowflakes? Words and thoughts carry a frequency. When the vibration of love and gratitude came into the water, the most beautiful crystals, perfect complex crystals, were formed, whereas when low vibration words like fear and hate came into the water, irregular incomplete crystals were created.

We must remember also to raise the vibration of the emotions and conversations that are happening during the meal. Every time you put something into your body, whether it is food or drink, consciously raise your vibration with loving thoughts. This will help raise the vibration of the food or drink. When lower vibrations resonate in the food or drink, your body may be affected, even causing hypersensitivity called allergies.

Blessing others in person or at a distance is a gift and it is free. Blessing the environment, home, office and world will help to raise the vibration everywhere, so that you can keep and raise your vibration higher. As each individual becomes aware to do this and give the gift of blessings, we will all feel healthier, more energetic and higher love.

Love and Gratitude,
Princess Mani

Multidimensional Healing

What is healing? The goal of healing is to return your body's energy to your original divine blueprint, releasing all that was not in the original blueprint. As this process occurs, you will experience more light energy in your body, peace and joy.

Begin your inner healing by letting go of negative thoughts and emotions soon after experiencing a stressful situation. Transmute the negative energy back to light. Let go of past negative memories. One's soul has journeyed a long time and some past memories may be held below your conscious awareness. Releasing the past memories and belief systems that cause dis-ease will increase healing.

Forgiveness is needed to release the negative energies from the past events that are held in the mind, emotions and body. Remember to forgive yourself, as well as others. Forgive yourself for creating any negative thoughts, feelings and actions. Purifying the mind means getting rid of all negative thinking. Let go of fear, criticism, complaints, competition, anger, blame, guilt, judgment, ego, etc. In addition to self-work, there are many tools and therapies to assist you, including affirmations, hypnotherapy and Spiritual Response Therapy.

One important reason why we came into incarnation was to heal. Heal the mind, body and spirit from present and past negative experiences that we are still carrying. If we do not heal these energies, they get carried forward into the future. As soon as you know there lies within you areas that wish to heal, allow yourself to feel and ask how it could be healed? If you have tried some common ways, but they did not clear the problem, consider finding out information about various holistic health practitioners. There can be energies in the subconscious mind and in the fascia of the body that are stuck and block your energy and health.

It is true that you have to feel in order to heal. Often, the pain or symptoms that come up get suppressed. It does not help you to heal by suppressing the symptoms, ignoring them, denying them, etc. Pain is a way the body communicates with you. Pain is an indication that there is something that needs to be examined and healed. We as humans were designed as super sensory beings, with the ability to sense disharmony. It serves you to listen within and keep asking "What is coming up?" and ask your higher self "What and who can help me to heal?"

Areas of blocked energy are past emotions and traumas in the body, and these will cause symptoms over time. An area that has been traumatized becomes blocked-off in feeling, conscious connection, hydration, nutrition and health. The energies from past emotional memories or traumatic events that got stuck in the crystalline matrix are still playing in the body, twenty-four hours a day and seven days a week. It serves you well to work with a Myofascial Release Therapist to clear these energies. If you are lucky enough to realize this and work with a therapist to clear your crystalline matrix, you can move forward more quickly on this healing journey.

Purify your food, water and environment as much as possible. When the body recognizes a foreign substance, like chemicals, it innately attempts to eliminate the invader. If it cannot, it tries to wall it off, creating a thwarted inflammatory response. The toxin is a stressor to the body and at times the body will experience an inflammatory response, signaling that it is still there. That area of thwarted inflammatory response remains, blocking energy flow until it can be released and healed.

Remember that what energy you are expressing, you are creating more of. Once the old blocked energy is cleared, you will feel lighter, brighter, joyful, and more like yourself. There may be a need for receiving assistance from a practitioner to clear the mind of false belief systems. Once you choose not to create anymore negative thoughts, let go of false belief systems in the mind, and clear the fascia of past emotional memories and traumas, you become a clear channel. This means you have a clear mind and pure heart to experience the fullness of giving and receiving, and have a greater ability to understand with wisdom and compassion. Joy and abundant energy will be available to you, which will help you create and manifest an abundant life.

Everyone's journey is different. What is blocked in your mind, body and spirit crystalline matrix is up to you to find out and clear. To let go of the blocked energy is to truly heal. Ask to know more about what lies within so you can get the kind of healing you need to become that pure, crystal vessel – your original divine blueprint.

Affirming your love and courage to heal.

Princess Mani

Kundalini Yoga and Meditation: Connect to your Higher Self

D ear ones, there is a tool I want to teach you that allows you to become more aware of your energy, mind, body, spirit and soul. It has been around for thousands of years, a practice called Kundalini Yoga. It was designed to yoke you to your higher self.

Kundalini yoga expands the potential creative life force that lies within you. Unless tapped into, the kundalini lies dormant at the base of the spine. Through breathwork and exercise, you can release the energy stored at the core and base of the spine, which allows it to flow through the central channel, in front of the spine to the crown. This expanded creative life force helps to open up compressed areas of the body, clarify the mind and purify negative emotions. With expanded creative energy flowing, a meditation is then practiced. This will connect you deeper to your soul. In this state of feeling inward, you begin to connect to your whole energetic body and your higher self.

In this zero point state of consciousness, you can ask questions in the form of prayer and receive answers to those questions. Intuition begins to flow, to guide you and give you answers to your questions. You do not have to seek answers for your soul outside of yourself if you have this practice. All the answers lie within, and they are the truest and highest answers for you.

Only your higher self knows your journey and all of what is going on. If you ask someone else for advice, he or she only has part of the information, so he or she cannot give you the highest answers for you. Sometimes it is helpful to talk things through with a trusted friend, family member or professional. Then, make sure you ask your higher self if it is the best decision that you could make. If not, there are setbacks. Ask some more questions and meditate on your prayer requests. If you do not get answers right away, know that they will come in other forms of communication shortly. Remember that English is not the communication of angels and all higher guides, so keep an open mind to learning and receiving other forms of communication.

You may wish to pick up a pendulum and see if it will respond to you. If it does, you are ready to use that tool to receive your higher self's yes or no responses to your questions. If you have mastered the use of a pendulum, you are ready to let go of the pendulum and feel the energy in your third eye energy center or heart energy center for the answer. It will have a motion like the pendulum that will give you the same answer. It is pretty amazing. The flow of energy from your higher self, which is high above you, to your physical body, comes in via your crown chakra and flows into your whole body. If you are holding a pendulum, this flow of energy flows through the heart chakra to your hand and transfers to the pendulum. If someone is doing kinesiology testing on your arm, your arm will respond, because it knows the answer to the question being asked by the tester. That answer in the form of energy comes from the subconscious mind and higher self.

The answers to the greater questions like, "What is my higher life purpose?" are held in the higher self. The most efficient and effective guidance to get there and manifest parts (and eventually the whole) can be accessed when you have a practice of yoga and meditation. Yoga then is a tool, and so is meditation, to connect you to your higher self. Build skills that you can add to your tool box so you can pick and choose what tools you need on a given day until you develop direct connection at all times. When you become conscious with everything – conscious seeing, conscious knowing and conscious asking – you begin to communicate telepathically with your higher self. From this point onward, the answers and guidance can happen automatically and simultaneously.

Great! Now you are on your way to experiencing more synchronicities and miracles. You will be able to manifest the small and the large mind creations on your higher path. Journeying through life being connected to your higher self is more blissful and makes you more successful.

Sat Nam in Kundalini Yoga means, truth identified. You will come to know, access and integrate your higher self, which is your divine truth. Also, you will be able to know the next step toward your higher life purpose, your truth to experience the greatest fulfillment in this lifetime.

Sat Nam,
Princess Mani

Present Living

Are you living in the present? If you are busy regretting events of the past or worrying about the future, you are creating stress, using up vital energy and not receiving the energy for the *now*. It is in the *now* that you can experience joy and love. By living in the present, you will be gifted with greater vitality, smiles and beauty.

In the now, you can be fully present for others and expand the ability to give and receive. In the now, you can better create what is in front of you. If you are all present, you will desire to be more creative, and the creativity will expand and flow into other areas of your life. Living in the present is living fully in the moment; you will not be left with regrets.

We know that hobbies are good for us. Once engaged in a hobby, you know you are in the moment. All of your focus shifts to the hobby. Hobbies are enjoyable and as you get into the hobby, time seems to disappear. If you do not have a hobby, consider starting one. If you have difficulty living each moment in the present, try the following short cut.

It is simple. Center yourself by feeling fully present in the body and clearing your mind of thoughts regarding the past or future. You can use deep breaths to help center yourself and clear the extraneous thoughts. Until it becomes a habit, consider it inner work and clear the thoughts not relevant to the present moment. A little inner work goes a long way and results in much happiness.

In the now, your mind and heart can be connected to your higher self. You can receive guidance and light. Having a meditation practice allows you to practice being in a still point, which translates to living consciously in the moment with divine flow. This can guide you with improved communication, introduce solutions and create flow into any present challenging life situation.

Once you begin to choose present living, you will not choose to go back. This is conscious living. Notice how everything improves from relationships, communication, energy, creativity, to your happiness. Try it today and receive the gift of today.

Divinely Present,
Princess Mani

Princess Mani
Purity

Purity of mind, purity of heart will lead to purity of everything else in your life. Purity is a higher vibration; return to the divine blueprint in which you were made. The divine blueprint is the energy of your higher self. The roadmap lies within.

If the mind, including the subconscious mind, has negative thoughts and emotions, just begin letting go of any negativity that comes to awareness. Choose not to allow that thought to stay in your mind. Choose not to allow the monkey mind to create any more negativity – allow a negative thought to stay in the mind only once. Do not let it loop through your mind more than once. You can allow it to come into the mind when you need it. The other times, catch yourself and block the negative thoughts.

Through practices like yoga, hypnotherapy, dream analysis, meditation, Spiritual Response Therapy and Myofascial Release, memories from deeper in the mind may come to awareness. Then they can be let go. It is much like flipping a light switch. It is quick and simple. The trick is to be consciously aware, know the process, trust and continue the process. Receive assistance from practitioners who can support and guide you with energy, love and healing.

Whenever you allow someone's negativity into your mind and you create negative thoughts, allowing the monkey mind to take over, you drop into a lower vibration. It then becomes harder to get out of that energy. It is like a fight or flight response happening in the subconscious mind all day, 24/7. You must forgive others, ask God to forgive you for your part in creating negative thoughts, and forgive yourself. This transforms the negative experience and energy back into the light. Remember that creating negative energy, whether in words or actions, is recorded and known in your Akashic Records. You are responsible for your thoughts, words and actions. The other person is responsible for his or her thoughts, words and actions. Later, there is a cause and effect experience that will come up as a consequence. Despite other people being negative towards you, be your highest self, clear the negativity and set it neutral in your mind and heart. Invoke the Violet Flame to transmute the negative energy. It is a choice, and when you relearn to operate from the soul space, it becomes easier to do.

Stressful or traumatic memories can get stuck in the connective tissues of the body, called fascia. It is a crystalline matrix. Visualize the most intricate, complex crystalline matrix. That is your physical body's vessel, which connects every cell to every other cell and every space in between, bathed and energetically bonded to living water. It sounds beautiful and amazing and it is truly the form in all living creatures and plants. In the crystalline matrix, even when you say I have no diseases, there still may be underlying negative emotions that resonate like anxiety, fear or sadness stuck in the matrix. We have all been subject to negative energies, for some of us negative verbal abuse and physical abuse, war, physical trauma and accidents.

If the heart center is blocked energetically with hurts from the past, it can be cleared and must be cleared for you to reconnect the heart to your mind. When there is purity of mind and an open heart, they work together to allow for divine receptivity, communication and connection to everything. Now you can regain your higher energy vibration and live a happier life. Know that despite the worst experiences in life, there is a way to clear them from your mind, body and spirit so you can return yourself to purity of mind and an open heart. Keep going forward in this process of purification. You are divine; you are crystal purity.

Peace & Love,
Princess Mani

Sound Current

The ancient ways always included using sound for spiritual and social events. You may have heard of chanting or mantra. These are becoming popular again as we relearn the benefits of listening and singing to them. Remember, we are crystal vessels, within every space in our physical bodies is liquid crystalline matrix. We are a fine instrument, one of the finest ever created. To keep it in good shape over time, we must tune it up. Singing and dancing are ways to do this. Energy can get stuck and compressed. If we sit for too long over time, we get back pain or other joint pains.

Find some high vibration music to play at home, such as yoga music, Reiki music, chanting, angelic music, Celtic music, sounds of nature, etc. You will know once you hear it because it will raise your vibration and you will like it. Consider playing this type of music in the background when you are home. It will raise the vibration of your home. If you have plants and animals at home, they will feel it too.

If you do not have animals, consider getting plants as pets. They are less maintenance, yet they are living and responsive. They also have a crystalline matrix in which consciousness flows. They give out oxygen and nature's frequency which is a relaxing, healing vibration. The plants will respond positively to the music's high vibrations with you.

When you sing, the music oscillates the vocal cords and the surrounding area. As you practice singing, allow the resonance to flow through all of the cells of your body. This can be a healing practice as it releases endorphins and clears some energetic blocks in the body. If you sit for a while, you may find emotions from the subconscious mind arise and release. Try it and feel it out; it is free and enjoyable.

Dancing in your own space at home can be a great way to clear the clutter of the mind and compression of the body collected from the day. Turn on a song and allow your body to feel the music, and for every cell to resonate to the music. Songs with a strong drumbeat are better for this purpose. Allow the rhythm to lead your movements. When you allow your whole body to move, you will feel lighter and be able to let dense and negative thoughts of the mind go, creating clarity of mind. It is a great way to end your day. Unwind your body, unwind your mind, clear the clutter and rest easy.

Let the music flow and dance like no one is watching. Care enough to treat your beautiful body instrument with all that it needs to resonate the highest and brightest energy. Life is sound in motion.

Enjoy the music and dancing.

Princess Mani

Access Higher Path with Higher Consciousness

Ignorance is no longer bliss. We have many habits that do not serve us. So much of what we do has become automatic pilot. Have you ever driven home and forgotten driving for a stretch of the road home? This is because your mind had checked out; it was not fully present. When we realize individually, then collectively, that things have strayed far from peace and harmony, it is time to awaken to conscious living.

Everything is a choice. We make many choices each day. Know that you are making choices. To shift into higher consciousness, ask yourself every day which activities to engage in and which activities to let go of. You really do not have to accomplish everything on your to-do list today. Eliminate distractions, whether habits or substances, for they only take away your creative energy and time and keep you from journeying forward on your higher path. Having a to-do list is constant pressure. Your higher self has access to more knowledge and a higher perspective. Also, ask your higher self for flow so you can be of service to others and to flow others into your life to help you.

You can learn to meditate simply by being still to ask for love, guidance and protection for this day. You must ask to know what is really important for today. Allow yourself to say *yes* to things on your higher path for today and *no* to those that are not on your higher path for today. You may find yourself saying no to more things, but find more peace and presence in your day. This practice of being more conscious and focused will allow you to begin, continue or accelerate the journey on your higher path.

We have been making choices every day of our lives, whether we know it or not. It is time to awaken to living more consciously. When your awareness expands, you realize your choices are infinite. There are so many roads to choose. Which ones will you choose, and in what sequence and timing? How will you choose? The navigation system lies within your higher self.

When you have driven around in circles, not arriving at your destiny, it is time to surrender the ego and connect to your soul which is connected to your higher self. Plug into your special GPS that will guide you with steps to get there. Remember, no one else has the navigation system to your destiny. You must develop communication access to your system. It is very easy because it comes prewired! Until you realize you have a higher self, you will be steering your life according to your ego, constantly reprogramming the GPS set to your higher life path. It is a great time for awakening to experience your higher life. Turn on the navigation system of your higher self. Enjoy the drive, the scenery and amazing connections and creations you are about to experience. This will continue as you fulfill your divine life purpose and manifest your higher destiny.

Godspeed,
Princess Mani

Relationships: You Are Love

Everyone wants to be loved. The greatest fear is not being loved, not being able to communicate or express love. Do you feel this way or know someone who does?

If you will start to release negative thoughts and emotions from the mind, love will grow. If only the people with the negative emotions, words and actions could see what they cause, they would stop because they would know that it is the opposite of love, and that the actual result is suffering to the other people who are being attacked with negativity. Most people wish for their families to have peace and love, yet they do not. Why? Individuals have to let go of negativity, negative thoughts, emotions and actions. They need to understand that every soul is different and cannot expect another soul to be alike, similar or the same.

When a person has negative energy, he or she will find someone meek who is in proximity to be the subject of negative energy attacks. Negative energy is like a vortex of energy that grows over time unless the person consciously chooses to change and let go of negative thoughts. If the person does not want to change or denies that there is anything wrong, then the negative energy builds over time, exploding out like a volcano at unexpected moments. The only thing certain is that it will happen again.

There is so much suffering in the world. The problem is simple to define and the problem is so simple to change. Surrender your will and realize you are responsible for any negative thoughts, words and actions you create. Realize that negative energy attacks have a deep negative impact for you and cause others deep suffering. Other people might not tell you because you will not listen, they are afraid of speaking up or they have disconnected.

Some people choose to leave the relationship if pushed away by negative energies too far, too long. They suffered long enough and want peace. It takes courage to walk away, especially when they have been shut down by the negative energies, losing self, voice, joy, creativity, hope, purpose and self-esteem. These negative energies are the opposite of love. When you get subjected to negativity long enough, you start to feel negative toward yourself and others. Depression is a sign of this inner feeling and mind chatter.

If the person attacking with negative energy would realize he or she is pushing love away, that person might choose to change. One can never find love with negative words and actions. If one carries on a long time, he or she develops a fear of not being loved and not being able to express love. This can have a ripple effect on the generations. It only takes a decision to make a change and then it can be transformed quickly.

If you say show me, I will tell you to release all negative thoughts that come in your mind regarding thoughts about others, thoughts about yourself and circumstances. Release each negative thought, one at a time. Keep cleansing of negative energy. Become an observer, a participant without judgment, criticism and condemnation. Learn to let go of thoughts before they lead to a judgment or loop around in your mind which is that negative energy vortex growing. Forgive, so you do not feel hatred or anger against another despite what he or she has done to you. It's important to do conscious clearing right away; do it as the thought comes in the first time. That is long enough to carry that negativity; breathe, let it go. Otherwise, repeated thinking or monkey mind creates more of the negative energy. Angry thoughts will breed more anger, and over time the anger will be uncontrollable and play out at an unconscious level. If you can stay connected to your heart space of compassion, there will be no outburst of negative attacks. There will be understanding and harmony.

Another lesson on truth is that every thought, word and action is seen, known and recorded in your Akashic Records. Please realize the truth and choose not to create any more negativity. It is your choice and responsibility. Know that in creating negative energy, there is a consequence that you may not see until much later. Know that anyone in your field and especially the person being attacked will be hurt, suffer and lose. We are all here to learn, grow and share. Remember the truth that we are all here to learn to love all, grow our ability to love all and share love with all.

Even if you need distance in a relationship, sending divine love from a distance can help the other individual increase his or her energy vibration. Of course the amount of change possible in a relationship depends on the individual surrendering and wanting to make a change to clear negativity. Never give up hope, yet protect your energy and create space as you need, to keep your energy from sinking low. Sometimes you can love someone more at a distance, and if that is the case, then choose that.

You want to maintain connection to your true self and to know your self-worth, which are human needs for soul freedom. Have hope, even from a distance, that someday that individual will transform to allow love to resonate and flow outward. When you pray, you can pray for this miracle to happen within that person's lifetime. Then release the thought. We do not have control over someone, but know that energetically, you can have a positive effect on them even at a distance. Choose to transform yourself from negativity in the way you think of the other person and choose to feel compassion and hope. Choose victory for your soul, and send prayers for the other person's victory. You will see more miracles in your life.

Do you see that our society has put the bottom line on money and outer things? Truly all that really matters in this life are the inner transformations you make that result in love and giving love. It's like turning the light switches from the off position of negativity to the on position where love happens naturally. Can you imagine the effect of the light switches flipping on more and more in your community, country and world? The peace, harmony and love that people want could be achieved sooner than later and what a wonderful world it would be.

Once you clear the negativity in mind, words and actions, you will feel more love for yourself and for others. Others will feel more love from you. Even when there is someone so different in your family, you could disagree and keep the peace. You could get along with others, respecting differences. Love is the pure state once the negativity is released. You do not have to seek love, it is within you. You do have to choose change; choose to let go of negativity in order to have more love. If you get in the habit of forgiving, you will carry less negative energy. You will find that letting go of the negativity and choosing forgiveness will lead you back to love and joy.

Know that any relationship can be healed this way. Once the negativity is gone, you know what to do. It comes naturally because it is your essence; it is who you are. You are Love. Enjoy turning on more lights and sharing this simple way of transforming negativity to love.

Sending you love,
Princess Mani

Relationships: You Are Your Own Energy

Maintain your presence in the body when engaged with others. Connect at heart center when you speak, but have your energy boundary intact so others do not drain your energy or you do not carry their energy. Feel and communicate, but maintain healthy energetic boundaries. If you sense these imbalances, let it go and try for better next time.

We are, after all, all energy. We can become conscious as to how best to share, grow and maintain our energies. With awareness, there is choice. Just by asking "What can I do to improve the balance of energy?" the relationship can get better. The answer will come through your intuition or through other pathways which we call synchronicity.

Everything has purpose, even pain and suffering. Know that once you have experienced it, you can begin to transform it. And in the transformation phase, you strengthen faith, patience and your connection to self. And from the transformation, on the other side of the bridge, you become greater than before in wisdom and spiritual evolution. You are evolving, and your capacity to help others and carry more light increases.

If you have any weaknesses or resistance to anything, those are the areas to grow into. If there are repetitious events or happenings, those are life lessons to learn. Remember everything is watched, known and recorded in Akashic records. Know that the greatest gain in life is transforming negativity to love, balancing negative karma (which means learning the life lessons), sharing your testimony and being the light for others.

We do affect others by our energy because all is energy. Learn to flow, let go of habits including business and to do lists. Learn to be in stillness and clear the chatter of the mind. Step outside of boxes and let go of fear and control mode. When you try to control your life to go according to how you want everything to go, it does not work out that way. We were meant to live with faith, trust, higher perspective and wisdom. Each one of us has a higher path, and to get there we have to allow the path to unfold through divine flow.

When you control versus allow life to unfold, you do not manifest your higher path. The key is to surrender resistance, control and fear. Allow flow, grace, feelings and new experiences in your life. Let go of habits, security blankets, and other things that hold you back. Those things could also be your false belief systems, self doubt and subconscious fears. Move away from being subject to others who inflict negativity onto you which causes you to feel small.

Sometimes we let go of relationships that hold us back, temporarily or permanently. Creating space can be an opportunity for positive change. We do not have to dwell on it because the future is undecided. Each person has free will so if each does inner work to release negativity which raises vibration, there could be harmony in the future and a chance for a closer relationship. Open communication with heart compassion can improve relationships with others and create a deeper connection to yourself.

Codependent relationships do not work out in the long run. It is a lose-lose relationship. Both lose self-sovereignty, freedom and manifesting higher purpose. Each soul has unique higher life purpose and needs space – full access to one's energetic field – in order to receive and integrate the information and carry it out.

The win-win relationship happens when two individuals can realize and actualize their own true selves and higher life purpose. Do not wait any longer to live your true life. Do not wait on another person or event to happen. You do not need anyone else but yourself to live fully with purpose. Your life is moving forward if you do this, regardless of whether you are engaged in a personal relationship or not.

If you are experiencing more joy, higher and newer life lessons and helping others more, you are expanding your light. The truest definition of success that I have come across is that it is the amount of light you carry. Does that give you a higher perspective? Knowing these truths will help you on your journey to your success.

Love and Light to your success.

Princess Mani

Stepping Onto the Stage of Creativity and Actualizing Your Creation

There are challenging times in life when you are guided to take baby steps, when there are many obstacles. There is always a way out of the obstacle course and back into freedom and flow. Prayer and meditation will give you information and guidance to the highest path out of the obstacle course. Remember that earth is a schoolhouse for the soul and we are in the process of releasing negative feelings and beliefs to become pure love and infinite in wisdom.

As you walk the journey of your life and remain in gratitude, trusting in your higher self, you will realize that you are not alone. The angels, guides and Ascended Masters walk with you. They are energetically present. They come in to teach, guide, bless and love you. Remember to draw them near with your love and conscious connection. When you remember them, you will feel more divine love and have more synchronistic experiences in each day.

To keep having these blessings, pray and meditate on each aspect of your life. This translates into conscious living. As you practice this, realize that you with your higher self make a super you. Access your higher self to make the best decisions for you. By living consciously, you realize there is even more to choose from. Actually, the choices are infinite. When you start to see life this way, you are in the flow of creation.

When you are ready, in your mind's eye, you will see doors open and later a stage will appear in front of you. This is an exciting time, a time to build and create. It may be fear that stops you from stepping up onto the stage because you do not think you can do it. Keep letting go of fear and know that you can learn each thing that is new to be learned along the pathway onto the stage, and know that you will be better than you imagine when you give your first performance on that stage.

Once you are willing to step onto the stage, the guidance, information, connections and empowerment will come flowing into your life. If there are any areas you feel weak in, and if you do not shy away from improving them, they can be transformed into strengths as you take the steps forward. You will be surprised and amazed at the abilities that lie dormant. With practice, you will shine, improving with each performance.

Creation is a gift to each human by our creator. We are born to create, and each soul, through the higher self, knows its destiny or higher life purpose. We must be open to creating in order to accomplish our destiny. First receive guidance from intuition. Gather information using the logical mind. Integrate the information from both sides of the brain. Feel the desired outcome, which will make you excited and hopeful. Then take the first step in creative action. If you let go of the outcome exactly as you imagined it happening, you will allow flow to help and optimize the manifestation.

If you find you are at a door and it does not open, step back and see what door does open for you. That is the divine flow guiding you. If there is a pause in the process, ask the meaning of this and wait for the guidance. It may be a time for learning or different action. Something greater maybe coming your way through another door or that other door that is closed now is not ready and will open at a later time.

There is no such thing as limitation and competition; those false beliefs are just a creation of human thinking. So it is in removing the fear of lack, as well as any other fears dwelling in your mind, that you will come to free yourself completely. Try conquering one fear at a time and keep going. Reprogram those thoughts into thoughts like these – there is infinite supply, Divine source is the source of all supply. It is then that you can tap into this divine love energy and begin to create new projects, partnerships, businesses and organizations that are enjoyable to you and help others.

Each creation will be unique, precious and awesome. Like a muscle, the more you practice and expand the use of creating works that bless you and other people, the better you will get at it.

Through this process, you will come to know how amazing living on earth can be because you are now creating Heaven on Earth as your higher desires are manifesting. No more monotony, lack of purposeful living, depression and drudgery. These words will be replaced by freedom, possibilities, passion, enthusiasm, collaboration, unity, service, faith, hope and love.

Enjoy creating and sharing your beautiful, loving creations!

Princess Mani

Miracles of
Living Crystals
of Light

You and I are living liquid crystals comprised of at least seventy percent crystal water. As you raise your vibration, through various ways, the water within resonates much higher. If the water you drink resonates higher, your vibration rises too. Everything matters from what you think, what you drink, what you eat, what relationships you choose and what you choose to do each day. So many choices, and everything matters.

There is a crystalline matrix within each person. It is the connective tissue or fascia. In living humans, animals and plants the fascia is hydrated, forming the crystalline matrix that allows us all to have instantaneous connection. In the human body, the crystalline matrix connects all 100 trillion cells together. The energy travels through the human body at super light speed.

We have an amazing, powerful fiber optics system in our body, a super conductor that allows us more access to intuition the higher vibration we carry. We can access the energy in the environment, from our higher self, and ultimately the universe and multiverse. The more you can clear from your crystalline matrix – as well as have practices that allow you to expand into more light and continue your spiritual growth –

the higher your energy frequency will be. This gives you more possibilities. This creates alignment for what you wish to manifest in your life. In this state, you attract less of the things you do not want to have in your life. You receive more information from the higher self for guidance, protection, wisdom and purpose.

We know that our water supplies are not the pristine purity they used to be. We need to be more conscious of what we can do to improve the purity of the water and environment. It has a deep impact on our health, expansion and possibilities. As you help to purify yourself, remember to help to purify the water and the environment which we call our home.

We are all interconnected and one affects the other. Bless the water, Mother Earth, the plants and creatures. Send love and spend time in nature. Learn ways to connect with others to take action to improve the conditions. No one can do it alone. We are so much more effective when we work together. The creativity would be phenomenal with so many minds creating solutions to problems that we face. Remember we all have divine creative powers and with conscious group energy, nothing is impossible. We make the impossible possible.

Our liquid crystalline matrix allows us much more than we thought we could be, do, feel and know. Know the truth in the physiology, the functionality and capability of the hardware you were given. There is much software, meaning energy that has yet to be downloaded. More will come to you as you raise your vibration using the tools, and follow through on intuitive messages with action. The quicker you follow intuition, the more intuition you will receive to accelerate you on your higher path.

As you remember and expand into your divine flow, life will no longer be the same. It will be more vibrant in living, loving colors, and you will experience a constant state of synchronicities and miracles.

Blessings of miracles,
Princess Mani

Bibliography

Andrews, Ted. *Animal Speak: The Spiritual & Magical Powers of Creatures Great & Small*. Woodbury, Minnesota: Llewellyn Publications, 2013.

Virtue, Doreen. *Angel Numbers 101: The Meaning of 111,123,444, and Other Number Sequences*. Calsbad, CA: Hay House, Inc., 2008.

www.ingramcontent.com/pod-product-compliance
Lightning Source LLC
Chambersburg PA
CBHW041358090426
42741CB00001B/10